# AMERICAN EDUCATION

*Its Men*

*Ideas*

*and*

*Institutions*

Advisory Editor

*Lawrence A. Cremin*
Frederick A. P. Barnard Professor of Education
Teachers College, Columbia University

# Self-Culture

## William Ellery Channing

ARNO PRESS & THE NEW YORK TIMES
*New York * 1969*

Reprint edition 1969 by Arno Press, Inc.

\*

Library of Congress Catalog Card No. 74-89163

\*

Manufactured in the United States of America

# Editorial Note

AMERICAN EDUCATION: *Its Men, Institutions and Ideas*
presents selected works of thought and scholarship that have
long been out of print or otherwise unavailable. Inevitably, such
works will include particular ideas and doctrines that have been
outmoded or superseded by more recent research. Nevertheless,
all retain their place in the literature, having influenced educa-
tional thought and practice in their own time and having provided
the basis for subsequent scholarship.

*Lawrence A. Cremin*
Teachers College

# Self-Culture

# SELF-CULTURE.

## AN ADDRESS INTRODUCTORY TO THE
## FRANKLIN LECTURES,

### DELIVERED AT BOSTON, SEPTEMBER,
### 1838.

## BY WILLIAM E. CHANNING.

BOSTON:
DUTTON AND WENTWORTH, PRINTERS.
1838.

At a meeting of the Executive Committee of the *"Franklin Lectures,"* holden November 8th, 1838, the following resolutions were unanimously adopted:

*Voted,* That the thanks of this Committee be presented to the Rev. WILLIAM E. CHANNING, for the interesting and valuable Lecture delivered by him, introductory to the *Seventh Course* of Franklin Lectures.

*Voted,* That Dr. Walter Channing, Hon. Jonathan Phillips, and Enoch Hobart, Esq., be a Committee to communicate the foregoing resolution, and request a copy for the press.

DAVID KIMBALL, *Secretary.*

-------

To Dr. WALTER CHANNING, Hon. JONATHAN PHILLIPS, and ENOCH HOBART, Esq.

*Gentlemen:*

I thank you for communicating to me the vote of the Executive Committee of the Franklin Lectures, and I place at your disposal the lecture which they have requested for publication.

Very truly, your friend,

WM. E. CHANNING.

THIS address was intended to make two lectures; but the author was led to abridge it and deliver it as one, partly by the apprehension, that some passages were too abstract for a popular address, partly to secure the advantages of presenting the whole subject at once and in close connection, and for other reasons which need not be named. Most of the passages, which were omitted, are now published. The author respectfully submits the discourse to those, for whom it was particularly intended, and to the public, in the hope, that it will at least bring a great subject before the minds of some, who may not as yet have given to it the attention it deserves.

# ADDRESS.

My respected friends :

By the invitation of the committee of arrangements for the Franklin lectures, I now appear before you to offer some remarks introductory to this course. My principal inducement for so doing is my deep interest in those of my fellow citizens, for whom these lectures are principally designed. I understood that they were to be attended chiefly by those, who are occupied by manual labor ; and, hearing this, I did not feel myself at liberty to decline the service, to which I had been invited. I wished by compliance to express my sympathy with this large portion of my race. I wished to express my sense of obligation to those, from whose industry and skill I derive almost all the

comforts of life. I wished still more to express
my joy in the efforts they are making for their own
improvement, and my firm faith in their success.
These motives will give a particular character and
bearing to some of my remarks. I shall speak
occasionally as among those who live by the labor
of their hands. But I shall not speak as one separated from them. I belong rightfully to the great
fraternity of working men. Happily in this community we all are bred and born to work ; and
this honorable mark, set on us all, should bind
together the various portions of the community.

I have expressed my strong interest in the mass
of the people ; and this is founded not on their
usefulness to the community so much as on what
they are in themselves. Their condition is indeed
obscure ; but their importance is not on this account a whit the less. The multitude of men
cannot from the nature of the case be distinguished ; for the very idea of distinction is, that a
man stands out from the multitude. They make
little noise and draw little notice in their narrow
spheres of action ; but still they have their full
proportion of personal worth and even of greatness. Indeed every man, in every condition, is
great. It is only our own diseased sight which
makes him little. A man is great as a man, be he
where or what he may. The grandeur of his nature turns to insignificance all outward distinctions.
His powers of intellect, of conscience, of love, of

knowing God, of perceiving the beautiful, of acting on his own mind, on outward nature, and on his fellow creatures, these are glorious prerogatives. Through the vulgar error of undervaluing what is common, we are apt indeed to pass these by as of little worth. But as in the outward creation, so in the soul, the common is the most precious. Science and art may invent splendid modes of illuminating the apartments of the opulent ; but these are all poor and worthless, compared with the common light which the sun sends into all our windows, which he pours freely, impartially over hill and valley, which kindles daily the eastern and western sky ; and so the common lights of reason, and conscience, and love are of more worth and dignity than the rare endowments which give celebrity to a few. Let us not disparage that nature which is common to all men ; for no thought can measure its grandeur. It is the image of God, the image even of his infinity, for no limits can be set to its unfolding. He who possesses the divine powers of the soul is a great being, be his place what it may. You may clothe him with rags, may immerse him in a dungeon, may chain him to slavish tasks. But he is still great. You may shut him out of your houses; but God opens to him heavenly mansions. He makes no show indeed in the streets of a splendid city ; but a clear thought, a pure affection, a resolute act of a virtuous will have a dignity of quite

another kind and far higher than accumulations of
brick and granite and plaster and stucco, however
cunningly put together, or though stretching far
beyond our sight. Nor is this all. If we pass
over this grandeur of our common nature, and turn
our thoughts to that comparative greatness, which
draws chief attention, and which consists in the
decided superiority of the individual to the general standard of power and character, we shall find
this as free and frequent a growth among the obscure and unnoticed as in more conspicuous walks
of life. The truly great are to be found every
where, nor is it easy to say, in what condition they
spring up most plentifully. Real greatness has
nothing to do with a man's sphere. It does not
lie in the magnitude of his outward agency, in the
extent of the effects which he produces. The
greatest men may do comparatively little abroad.
Perhaps the greatest in our city at this moment
are buried in obscurity. Grandeur of character
lies wholly in force of soul, that is, in the force of
thought, moral principle and love, and this may
be found in the humblest condition of life. A man
brought up to an obscure trade, and hemmed in
by the wants of a growing family, may, in his narrow sphere, perceive more clearly, discriminate
more keenly, weigh evidence more wisely, seize
on the right means more decisively, and have
more presence of mind in difficulty, than another
who has accumulated vast stores of knowledge by

laborious study ; and he has more of intellectual greatness. ˘ Many a man, who has gone but a few miles from home, understands human nature better, detects motives and weighs character more sagaciously, than another, who has travelled over the known world, and made a name by his reports of different countries. It is force of thought which measures intellectual, and so it is force of principle which measures moral greatness, that highest of human endowments*, that brightest manifestation of the Divinity. The greatest man is he who chooses the Right with invincible resolution, who resists the sorest temptations from within and without, who bears the heaviest burdens cheerfully, who is calmest in storms and most fearless under menace and frowns, whose reliance on truth, on virtue, on God is most unfaltering ; and is this a greatness, which is apt to make a show, or which is most likely to abound in conspicuous station ? The solemn conflicts of reason with passion ; the victories of moral and religious principle over urgent and almost irresistible solicitations to self-indulgence ; the hardest sacrifices of duty, those of deep-seated affection and of the heart's fondest hopes ; the consolations, hopes, joys, and peace of disappointed, persecuted, scorned, deserted virtue ; these are of course unseen ; so that the true greatness of human life is almost wholly out of sight. Perhaps in our presence, the most heroic deed on earth is done in

2

some silent spirit, the loftiest purpose cherished, the most generous sacrifice made, and we do not suspect it. I believe this greatness to be most common among the multitude, whose names are never heard. Among common people will be found more of hardship borne manfully, more of unvarnished truth, more of religious trust, more of that generosity which gives what the giver needs himself, and more of a wise estimate of life and death, than among the more prosperous.—And even in regard to influence over other beings, which is thought the peculiar prerogative of distinguished station, I believe, that the difference between the conspicuous and the obscure does not amount to much. Influence is to be measured, not by the extent of purpose it covers, but by its *kind*. A man may spread his mind, his feelings and opinions through a great extent ; but if his mind be a low one, he manifests no greatness. A wretched artist may fill a city with daubs, and by a false showy style achieve a reputation ; but the man of genius, who leaves behind him one grand picture, in which immortal beauty is embodied, and which is silently to spread a true taste in his art, exerts an incomparably higher influence. Now the noblest influence on earth is that exerted on character; and he, who puts forth this, does a great work, no matter how narrow or obscure his sphere. The father and mother of an unnoticed family who, in their seclusion, awaken the mind of one child to the idea and love of perfect goodness, who awaken in him a strength of will to repel all temptation, and who send him out prepared to profit by the conflicts of life, surpass in influence a Napoleon breaking the world to his sway. And not only is their work higher in kind; who knows, but that they are doing a greater work even as to extent or surface than the conqueror? Who knows, but that the being, whom they inspire with holy and disinterested principles, may communicate himself to others; and that by a spreading agency, of which they were the silent origin, improvements may spread through a nation, through the world? In these remarks you will see why I feel and express a deep interest in the obscure, in the mass of men. The distinctions of society vanish before the light of these truths. I attach myself to the multitude, not because they are voters and have political power; but because they are men, and have within their reach the most glorious prizes of humanity.

In this country the mass of the people are distinguished by possessing means of improvement, of self-culture, possessed no where else. To incite them to the use of these, is to render them the best service they can receive. Accordingly I have chosen for the subject of this lecture, Self-culture, or the care which every man owes to himself, to the unfolding and perfecting of his nature. I consider this topic as particularly appropriate to the introduction of a course of lectures, in consequence of a common disposition to regard these and other like means of instruction, as able of themselves to carry forward the hearer. Lectures have their use. They stir up many, who, but for such outward appeals, might have slumbered to the end of life. But let it be remembered, that little is to be gained simply by coming to this place once a week, and giving up the mind for an hour to be wrought upon by a teacher. Unless we are roused to act upon ourselves, unless we engage in the work of self-improvement, unless we purpose strenuously to form and elevate our own minds, unless what we hear is made a part of ourselves by conscientious reflection, very little permanent good is received.

Self-culture, I am aware, is a topic too extensive for a single discourse, and I shall be able to present but a few views which seem to me most important. My aim will be, to give first the Idea of self-culture, next its Means, and then to consider some objections to the leading views which I am now to lay before you.

Before entering on the discussion, let me offer one remark. Self-culture is something possible. It is not a dream. It has foundations in our nature. Without this conviction, the speaker will but declaim, and the hearer listen without profit. There are two powers of the human soul which make self-culture possible, the self-searching and the self-forming power. We have first the faculty of turning the mind on itself; of recalling its past, and watching its present operations; of learning its various capacities and susceptibilities, what it can do and bear, what it can enjoy and suffer ; and of thus learning in general what our nature is, and what it was made for. It is worthy of observation, that we are able to discern not only what we already are, but what we may become, to see in ourselves germs and promises of a growth to which no bounds can be set, to dart beyond what we have actually gained to the idea of Perfection as the end of our being. It is by this self-comprehending power that we are distinguished from the brutes, which give no signs of looking into themselves. Without this there would be no self-culture, for we should not know the work to be done; and one reason why self-culture is so little proposed is, that so few penetrate into their own nature. To most men, their own spirits are shadowy, unreal, compared with what is outward. When they happen to cast a glance inward, they see there only a dark, vague chaos. They distinguish perhaps some violent passion, which has driven them to injurious excess ; but their highest powers hardly attract a thought ; and thus multitudes live and die as truly strangers to themselves, as to countries, of which they have heard the name, but which human foot has never trodden.

But self-culture is possible, not only because we

can enter into and search ourselves. We have a still nobler power, that of acting on, determining and forming ourselves. This is a fearful as well as glorious endowment, for it is the ground of human responsibility. We have the power not only of tracing our powers, but of guiding and impelling them, not only of watching our passions, but of controlling them, not only of seeing our faculties grow, but of applying to them means and influences to aid their growth. We can stay or change the current of thought. We can concentrate the intellect on objects which we wish to comprehend. We can fix our eyes on perfection and make almost every thing speed us towards it. This is indeed a noble prerogative of our nature. Possessing this, it matters little what or where we are now, for we can conquer a better lot, and even be happier for starting from the lowest point. Of all the discoveries which men need to make, the most important at the present moment, is that of the self-forming power treasured up in themselves. They little suspect its extent, as little as the savage apprehends the energy which the mind is created to exert on the material world. It transcends in importance all our power over outward nature. There is more of divinity in it, than in the force which impels the outward universe ; and yet how little we comprehend it! How it slumbers in most men unsuspected, unused! This makes self-culture possible, and binds it on us as a solemn duty.

I. I am first to unfold the idea of self-culture; and this, in its most general form, may easily be seized. To cultivate any thing, be it a plant, an animal, a mind, is to make grow. Growth, expansion is the end. Nothing admits culture, but that which has a principle of life, capable of being expanded. He, therefore, who does what he can to unfold all his powers and capacities, especially his nobler ones, so as to become a well proportioned, vigorous, excellent, happy being, practises self-culture.

This culture of course has various branches corresponding to the different capacities of human nature; but though various, they are intimately united and make progress together. The soul which our philosophy divides into various capacities, is still one essence, one life; and it exerts at the same moment, and blends in the same act its various energies of thought, feeling and volition. Accordingly in a wise self-culture all the principles of our nature grow at once by joint harmonious action, just as all parts of the plant are unfolded together. When therefore you hear of different branches of self-improvement, you will not think of them as distinct processes going on independently on each other, and requiring each its own separate means. Still a distinct consideration of these is needed to a full comprehension of the subject, and these I shall proceed to unfold.

First, self-culture is Moral, a branch of singular importance. When a man looks into himself he discovers two distant orders or kinds of principles, which it behoves him especially to comprehend. He discovers desires, appetites, passions which terminate in himself, which crave and seek his own interest, gratification, distinction; and he discovers another principle, an antagonist to these, which is Impartial, Disinterested, Universal, enjoining on him a regard to the rights and happiness of other beings, and laying on him obligations which *must* be discharged, cost what they may, or however they may clash with his particular pleasure or gain. No man, however narrowed to his own interest, however hardened by selfishness, can deny, that there springs up within him a great idea in opposition to interest, the idea of Duty, that an inward voice calls him more or less distinctly to revere and exercise Impartial Justice, and Universal Good-will. This disinterested principle in human nature we call sometimes reason, sometimes conscience, sometimes the moral sense or faculty. But, be its name what it may, it is a real principle in each of us, and it is the supreme power within us, to be cultivated above all others, for on its culture the right development of all others depends. The passions indeed may be stronger than the conscience, may lift up a louder voice; but their clamour differs wholly from the tone of command in which the conscience speaks. They are not clothed with its authority, its binding power. In their very triumphs they are rebuked by the moral principle, and often cower before its still deep menacing voice. No part of self-knowledge is more important than to discern clearly these two great principles, the self-seeking and the disinterested; and the most important part of self-culture is to depress the former, and to exalt the latter, or to enthrone the sense of duty within us. There are no limits to the growth of this moral force in man, if he will cherish it faithfully. There have been men, whom no power in the universe could turn from the Right, to whom death in its most dreadful forms has been less dreaded, than transgression of the inward law of universal justice and love.

In the next place, self-culture is Religious. When we look into ourselves we discover powers, which link us with this outward, visible, finite, ever changing world. We have sight and other senses to discern, and limbs and various faculties to secure and appropriate the material creation. And we have too a power, which cannot stop at what we see and handle, at what exists within the bounds of space and time, which seeks for the Infinite, Uncreated cause, which cannot rest till it ascend to the Eternal, All-comprehending Mind. This we call the religious principle, and its grandeur cannot be exaggerated by human language; for it marks out a being destined for higher communion than with the visible universe. To develope this, is eminently to educate ourselves. The

3

true idea of God, unfolded clearly and livingly within us, and moving us to adore and obey him, and to aspire after likeness to him, is the noblest growth in human, and I may add, in celestial natures. The religious principle, and the moral, are intimately connected, and grow together. The former is indeed the perfection and highest manifestation of the latter. They are both disinterested. It is the essence of true religion to recognize and adore in God the attributes of Impartial Justice and Universal Love, and to hear him commanding us in the conscience to become what we adore.

Again. Self-culture is Intellectual. We cannot look into ourselves without discovering the intellectual principle, the power which thinks, reasons, and judges, the power of seeking and acquiring truth. This indeed we are in no danger of overlooking. The intellect being the great instrument. by which men compass their wishes, it draws more attention than any of our other powers. When we speak to men of improving themselves, the first thought which occurs to them is, that they must cultivate their understanding, and get knowledge and skill. By education, men mean almost exclusively intellectual training. For this, schools and colleges are instituted, and to this the moral and religious discipline of the young is sacrificed. Now I reverence, as much as any man, the intellect; but let us never exalt it above the moral principle. With this it is most intimately connected. In this its culture is founded, and to exalt this is its highest aim. Whoever desires that his intellect may grow up to soundness, to healthy vigour, must begin with moral discipline. Reading and study are not enough to perfect the power of thought. One thing above all is needful, and that is, the Disinterestedness which is the very soul of virtue. To gain truth, which is the great object of the understanding, I must seek it disinterestedly. Here is the first and grand condition of intellectual progress. I must choose to receive the truth, no matter how it bears on myself. I must follow it, no matter where it leads, what interests it opposes, to what persecution or loss it lays me open, from what party it severs me, or to what party it allies. Without this fairness of mind, which is only another phrase for disinterested love of truth, great native powers of understanding are perverted and lead astray ; genius runs wild ; " the light within us becomes darkness." The subtlest reasoners, for want of this, cheat themselves as well as others, and become entangled in the web of their own sophistry. It is a fact well known in the history of science and philosophy, that men, gifted by nature with singular intelligence, have broached the grossest errors, and even sought to undermine the grand primitive truths on which human virtue, dignity and hope depend. And on the other hand, I have known instances of men of naturally moderate powers of mind, who by a disinterested love of truth and their fellow creatures, have gradually risen to no small force and enlargement of thought. Some of the most useful teachers in the pulpit and in schools, have owed their power of enlightening others, not so much to any natural superiority, as to the simplicity, impartiality and disinterestedness of their minds, to their readiness to live and die for the truth. A man, who rises above himself, looks from an eminence on nature and providence, on society and life. Thought expands as by a natural elasticity, when the pressure of selfishness is removed. The moral and religious principles of the soul, generously cultivated, fertilize the intellect. Duty, faithfully performed, opens the mind to Truth, both being of one family, alike immutable, universal and everlasting.

I have enlarged on this subject, because the connexion between moral and intellectual culture is often overlooked, and because the former is often sacrificed to the latter. The exaltation of talent, as it is called, above virtue and religion, is the curse of the age. Education is now chiefly a stimulus to learning, and thus men acquire power without the principles which alone make it a good. Talent is worshipped; but, if divorced from rectitude, it will prove more of a demon than a God.

Intellectual culture consists, not chiefly, as many are apt to think, in accumulating information,

though this is important, but in building up a force
of thought which may be turned at will on any
subjects, on which we are called to pass judgment.
This force is manifested in the concentration of the
attention, in accurate penetrating observation, in re-
ducing complex subjects to their elements, in diving
beneath the effect to the cause, in detecting the more
subtle differences and resemblances of things, in
reading the future in the present, and especially in
rising from particular facts to general laws or universal truths. This last exertion of the intellect, its
rising to broad views and great principles, con-
stitutes what is called the philosophical mind, and
is especially worthy of culture. What it means
your own observation must have taught you. You
must have taken note of two classes of men, the
one always employed on details, on particular
facts, and the other using these facts as foundations
of higher, wider truths. The latter are philoso-
phers. For example, men had for ages seen pieces
of wood, stones, metals falling to the ground.
Newton seized on these particular facts, and rose
to the idea, that all matter tends, or is attracted,
towards all matter, and then defined the law according to which this attraction or force acts at different distances, thus giving us a grand principle, which, we have reason to think, extends to and
controls the whole outward creation. One man
reads a history, and can tell you all its events,
and there stops. Another combines these events,

brings them under one view and learns the great causes which are at work on this or another nation, and what are its great tendencies, whether to freedom or despotism, to one or another form of civilization. So one man talks continually about the particular actions of this or another neighbour ; whilst another looks beyond the acts to the inward principle from which they spring, and gather from them larger views of human nature. In a word, one man sees all things apart and in fragments, whilst another strives to discover the harmony, connection, unity of all. One of the great evils of society is, that men, occupied perpetually with petty details, want general truths, want broad and fixed principles. Hence many, not wicked, are unstable, habitually inconsistent, as if they were overgrown children rather than men. To build up that strength of mind, which apprehends and cleaves to great universal truths, is the highest intellectual self-culture ; and here I wish you to observe how entirely this culture agrees with that of the moral and the religious principles of our nature, of which I have previously spoken. In each of these, the improvement of the soul consists in raising it above what is narrow, particular, individual, selfish, to the universal and unconfined. To improve a man, is to liberalize, enlarge him in thought, feeling and purpose. Narrowness of intellect and heart, this is the degradation from which all culture aims to rescue the human being.

Again. Self-culture is Social, or one of its great offices is to unfold and purify the affections, which spring up instinctively in the human breast, which bind together husband and wife, parent and child, brother and sister ; which bind a man to friends and neighbors, to his country, and to the suffering who fall under his eye, wherever they belong. The culture of these is an important part of our work, and it consists in converting them from instincts into principles, from natural into spiritual attachments, in giving them a rational, moral, and holy character. For example, our affection for our children is at first instinctive ; and if it continue such, it rises little above the brute's attachment to its young. But when a parent infuses into his natural love for his offspring moral and religious principle, when he comes to regard his child as an intelligent, spiritual, immortal being, and honors him as such, and desires first of all to make him disinterested, noble, a worthy child of God and the friend of his race, then the instinct rises into a generous and holy sentiment. It resembles God's paternal love for his spiritual family. A like purity and dignity we must aim to give to all our affections.

Again. Self-culture is Practical, or it proposes as one of its chief ends to fit us for action, to make us efficient in whatever we undertake, to train us to firmness of purpose and to fruitfulness of resource in common life, and especially in emergencies, in times of difficulty, danger and trial. But passing over this and other topics for which I have no time, I shall confine myself to two branches of self-culture which have been almost wholly overlooked in the education of the people, and which ought not to be so slighted.

In looking at our nature, we discover, among its admirable endowments, the sense or perception of Beauty. We see the germ of this in every human being; and there is no power which admits greater cultivation; and why should it not be cherished in all? It deserves remark, that the provision for this principle is infinite in the universe. There is but a very minute portion of the creation which we can turn into food and clothes, or gratification for the body; but the whole creation may be used to minister to the sense of beauty. Beauty is an all-pervading presence. It unfolds in the numberless flowers of the spring. It waves in the branches of the trees and the green blades of grass. It haunts the depths of the earth and sea, and gleams out in the hues of the shell and the precious stone. And not only these minute objects, but the ocean, the mountains, the clouds, the heavens, the stars, the rising and setting sun, all overflow with beauty. The universe is its temple; and those men who are alive to it cannot lift their eyes without feeling themselves encompassed with it on every side.

Now this beauty is so precious, the enjoyments it gives are so refined and pure, so congenial with our tenderest and noble feelings, and so akin to worship, that it is painful to think of the multitude of men as living in the midst of it, and living almost as blind to it, as if, instead of this fair earth and glorious sky, they were tenants of a dungeon.　An infinite joy is lost to the world by the want of culture of this spiritual endowment. Suppose that I were to visit a cottage, and to see its walls lined with the choicest pictures of Raphael, and every spare nook filled with statues of the most exquisite workmanship, and that I were to learn, that neither man, woman nor child ever cast an eye at these miracles of art, how should I feel their privation ; how should I want to open their eyes, and to help them to comprehend and feel the loveliness and grandeur which in vain courted their notice.　But every husbandman is living in sight of the works of a diviner artist ; and how much would his existence be elevated, could he see the glory which shines forth in their forms, hues, proportions and moral expression !　I have spoken only of the beauty of nature, but how much of this mysterious charm is found in the elegant arts, and especially in literature ?　The best books have most beauty.　The greatest truths are wronged if not linked with beauty, and they win their way most surely and deeply into the soul when arrayed in this their natural and fit attire. Now no man receives the true culture of a man, in whom the sensibility to the beautiful is not cherished; and I know of no condition in life from which it should be excluded. Of all luxuries this is the cheapest and most at hand; and it seems to me to be most important to those conditions, where coarse labor tends to give a grossness to the mind. From the diffusion of the sense of beauty in ancient Greece, and of the taste for music in modern Germany, we learn that the people at large, may partake of refined gratifications which have hitherto been thought to be necessarily restricted to a few.

What beauty is, is a question which the most penetrating minds have not satisfactorily answered; nor, were I able, is this the place for discussing it. But one thing I would say; the beauty of the outward creation is intimately related to the lovely, grand, interesting attributes of the soul. It is the emblem or expression of these. Matter becomes beautiful to us, when it seems to lose its material aspect, its inertness, finiteness and grossness, and by the ethereal lightness of its forms and motions seems to approach spirit; when it images to us pure and gentle affections; when it spreads out into a vastness which is a shadow of the Infinite; or when in more awful shapes and movements it speaks of the Omnipotent. Thus outward beauty is akin to something deeper and unseen, is the reflection of spiritual attributes;

and of consequence the way to see and feel it more and more keenly is to cultivate those moral, religious, intellectual and social principles of which I have already spoken, and which are the glory of the spiritual nature ; and I name this, that you may see, what I am anxious to show, the harmony which subsists among all branches of human culture, or how each forwards and is aided by all.

There is another power, which each man should cultivate according to his ability, but which is very much neglected in the mass of the people, and that is the power of Utterance. A man was not made to shut up his mind in itself; but to give it voice and to exchange it for other minds. Speech is one of our grand distinctions from the brute. Our power over others lies not so much in the amount of thought within us, as in the power of bringing it out. A man of more than ordinary intellectual vigor, may, for want of expression, be a cypher, without significance, in society. And not only does a man influence others, but he greatly aids his own intellect, by giving distinct and forcible utterance to his thoughts. We understand ourselves better, our conceptions grow clearer, by the very effort to make them clear to another. Our social rank too depends a good deal on our power of utterance. The principal distinction between what are called gentlemen and the vulgar lies in this, that the lat-

ter are awkward in manners, and are essentially
wanting in propriety, clearness, grace, and force
of utterance. A man who cannot open his lips
without breaking a rule of grammar, without
showing in his dialect or brogue or uncouth tones
his want of cultivation, or without darkening his
meaning by a confused, unskilful mode of communication, cannot take the place to which perhaps
his native good sense entitles him. To have intercourse with respectable people, we must speak
their language. On this account, I am glad that
grammar and a correct pronunciation are taught in
the common schools of this city. These are not
trifles ; nor are they superfluous to any class of
people. They give a man access to social advantages, on which his improvement very much depends. The power of utterance should be in-
cluded by all in their plans of self-culture.

I have now given a few views of the culture,
the improvement, which every man should pro-
pose to himself. I have all along gone on the
principle, that a man has within him capacities of
growth, which deserve and will reward intense,
unrelaxing toil. I do not look on a human being
as a machine, made to be kept in action by a foreign force, to accomplish an unvarying succession
of motions, to do a fixed amount of work, and then
to fall to pieces at death, but as a being of free spiritual powers ; and I place little value on any cul-

ture, but that which aims to bring out these and to
give them perpetual impulse and expansion. I
am aware, that this view is far from being universal. The common notion has been, that the mass
of the people need no other culture than is necessary to fit them for their various trades ; and
though this error is passing away, it is far from
being exploded. But the ground of a man's culture lies in his nature, not in his calling. His
powers are to be unfolded on account of their
inherent dignity, not their outward direction. He
is to be educated, because he is a man, not
because he is to make shoes, nails, or pins. A
trade is plainly not the great end of his being, for
his mind cannot be shut up in it ; his force of
thought cannot be exhausted on it. He has faculties to which it gives no action, and deep wants it
cannot answer. Poems, and systems of theology
and philosophy, which have made some noise in
the world, have been wrought at the work-bench
and amidst the toils of the field. How often,
when the arms are mechanically plying a trade,
does the mind, lost in reverie or day dreams,
escape to the ends of the earth ! How often does
the pious heart of woman mingle the greatest of
all thoughts, that of God, with household drudgery!
Undoubtedly a man is to perfect himself in his
trade, for by it he is to earn his bread and to
serve the community. But bread or subsistence
is not his highest good ; for if it were, his lot

would be harder than that of the inferior animals, for whom nature spreads a table and weaves a wardrobe, without a care of their own. Nor was he made chiefly to minister to the wants of the community. A rational moral being cannot without infinite wrong be converted into a mere instrument of others' gratification. He is necessarily an end, not a means. A mind, in which are sown the seeds of wisdom, disinterestedness, firmness of purpose, and piety, is worth more than all the outward material interests of a world. It exists for itself, for its own perfection, and must not be enslaved to its own or others' animal wants. You tell me, that a liberal culture is needed for men who are to fill high stations, but not for such as are doomed to vulgar labor. I answer, that Man is a greater name than President or King. Truth and goodness are equally precious, in whatever sphere they are found. Besides, men of all conditions sustain equally the relations, which give birth to the highest virtues and demand the highest powers. The laborer is not a mere laborer. He has close, tender, responsible connections with God and his fellow creatures. He is a son, husband, father, friend and Christian. He belongs to a home, a country, a church, a race ; and is such a man to be cultivated only for a trade ? Was he not sent into the world for a great work. To educate a child perfectly requires profounder thought, greater wisdom, than to govern a state ;

and for this plain reason, that the interests and
wants of the latter are more superficial, coarser,
and more obvious, than the spiritual capacities,
the growth of thought and feeling, and the subtle
laws of the mind, which must all be studied and
comprehended, before the work of education can
be thoroughly performed ; and yet to all conditions this greatest work on earth is equally com-
mitted by God. What plainer proof do we need
that a higher culture, than has yet been dreamt
of, is needed by our whole race.

II.   I now proceed to enquire into the Means
by which the self-culture, just described, may be
promoted; and here I know not where to begin.
The subject is so extensive, as well as important,
that I feel myself unable to do any justice to it,
especially in the limits to which I am confined.
I beg you to consider me as presenting but hints,
and such as have offered themselves with very
little research to my own mind.

And, first, the great means of self-culture, that
which includes all the rest, is to fasten on this
culture as our Great End, to determine deliberately and solemnly, that we will make the most
and the best of the powers which God has given
us. Without this resolute purpose, the best means
are worth little, and with it the poorest become
mighty. You may see thousands, with every
opportunity of improvement which wealth can

gather, with teachers, libraries, and apparatus, bringing nothing to pass, and others, with few helps, doing wonders; and simply because the latter are in earnest, and the former not. A man in earnest finds means, or, if he cannot find, creates them. A vigorous purpose makes much out of little, breathes power into weak instruments, disarms difficulties, and even turns them into assistances. Every condition has means of progress, if we have spirit enough to use them. Some volumes have recently been published, giving examples or histories of "knowledge acquired under difficulties;" and it is most animating to see in these what a resolute man can do for himself. A great idea, like this of Self-culture, if seized on clearly and vigorously, burns like a living coal in the soul. He who deliberately adopts a great end, has, by this act, half accomplished it, has scaled the chief barrier to success.

One thing is essential to the strong purpose of self-culture now insisted on, namely, faith in the practicableness of this culture. A great object, to awaken resolute choice, must be seen to be within our reach. The truth, that progress is the very end of our being, must not be received as a tradition, but comprehended and felt as a reality. Our minds are apt to pine and starve, by being imprisoned within what we have already attained. A true faith, looking up to something better, catching glimpses of a distant perfection, prophesying to ourselves improvements proportioned to our conscientious labors, gives energy of purpose, gives wings to the soul; and this faith will continually grow, by acquainting ourselves with our own nature, and with the promises of divine help and immortal life which abound in revelation.

Some are discouraged from proposing to themselves improvement, by the false notion, that the study of books, which their situation denies them, is the all important, and only sufficient means. Let such consider, that the grand volumes, of which all our books are transcripts, I mean, nature, revelation, the human soul, and human life, are freely unfolded to every eye. The great sources of wisdom are experience and observation; and. these are denied to none. To open and fix our eyes upon what passes without and within us, is the most fruitful study. Books are chiefly useful, as they help us to interpret what we see and experience. When they absorb men, as they sometimes do, and turn them from observation of nature and life, they generate a learned folly, for which the plain sense of the laborer could not be exchanged but at great loss. It deserves attention that the greatest men have been formed without the studies, which at present are thought by many most needful to improvement. Homer, Plato, Demosthenes, never heard the name of chemistry, and knew less of the solar system, than a boy in our common schools. Not that these sciences are unimportant; but the lesson is, that human improvement never wants the means, where the purpose of it is deep and earnest in the soul.

The purpose of self-culture, this is the life and strength of all the methods we use for our own elevation. I reiterate this principle on account of its great importance; and I would add a remark to prevent its misapprehension. When I speak of the purpose of self-culture, I mean, that it should be sincere. In other words, we must make self-culture really and truly our end, or choose it for its own sake, and not merely as a means or instrument of something else. And here I touch a common and very pernicious error. Not a few persons desire to improve themselves only to get property and to rise in the world; but such do not properly choose improvement, but something outward and foreign to themselves; and so low an impulse can produce only a stinted, partial, uncertain growth. A man, as I have said, is to cultivate himself because he is a man. He is to start with the conviction, that there is something greater within him than in the whole material creation, than in all the worlds which press on the eye and ear; and that inward improvements have a worth and dignity in themselves, quite distinct from the power they give over outward things. Undoubtedly a man is to labor to better his condition, but first to better himself. If he knows no higher use of his mind than to invent and drudge for his body, his case is desperate as far as culture is concerned.

In these remarks, I do not mean to recommend to the laborer indifference to his outward lot. I hold it important, that every man in every class should possess the means of comfort, of health, of neatness in food and apparel, and of occasional retirement and leisure. These are good in themselves, to be sought for their own sakes, and still more, they are important means of the self-culture for which I am pleading. A clean, comfortable dwelling, with wholesome meals, is no small aid to intellectual and moral progress. A man living in a damp cellar or a garret open to rain and snow, breathing the foul air of a filthy room, and striving without success to appease hunger on scanty or unsavoury food, is in danger of abandoning himself to a desperate, selfish recklessness. Improve then your lot. Multiply comforts, and still more get wealth if you can by honorable means, and if it do not cost too much. A true cultivation of the mind is fitted to forward you in your worldly concerns, and you ought to use it for this end. Only, beware, lest this end master you; lest your motives sink as your condition improves; lest you fall victims to the miserable passion of vying with those around you in show, luxury and expense. Cherish a true respect for yourselves. Feel that your nature is worth more than every thing which is foreign to you. He who has not caught a glimpse of his own rational and spiritual being, of something within himself superior to the world

and allied to the divinity, wants the true spring of
that purpose of self-culture, on which I have insisted as the first of all the means of improvement.

I proceed to another important means of Self-
culture, and this is the control of the animal appetites. To raise the moral and intellectual nature,
we must put down the animal. Sensuality is the
abyss in which very many souls are plunged and
lost. Among the most prosperous classes, what a
vast amount of intellectual life is drowned in lux-
urious excesses. It is one great curse of wealth,
that it is used to pamper the senses; and among
the poorer classes, though luxury is wanting, yet
a gross feeding often prevails, under which the
spirit is whelmed. It is a sad sight to walk through
our streets, and to see how many countenances
bear marks of a lethargy and a brutal coarseness,
induced by unrestrained indulgence. Whoever
would cultivate the soul, must restrain the appetites. I am not an advocate for the doctrine, that
animal food was not meant for man ; but that this
is used among us to excess, that as a people we
should gain much in cheerfulness, activity, and
buoyancy of mind, by less gross and stimulating
food, I am strongly inclined to believe. Above
all, let me urge on those, who would bring out and
elevate their higher nature, to abstain.from the
use of spirituous liquors. This bad habit is distinguished from all others by the ravages it makes

on the reason, the intellect ; and this effect is
produced to a mournful extent, even when drunk-
enness is escaped. Not a few men, called tempe-
rate, and who have thought themselves such, have
learned, on abstaining from the use of ardent
spirits, that for years their minds had been cloud-
ed, impaired by moderate drinking, without their
suspecting the injury. Multitudes in this city are
bereft of half their intellectual energy, by a degree
of indulgence which passes for innocent. Of all
the foes of the working class, this is the deadliest.
Nothing has done more to keep down this class,
to destroy their self-respect, to rob them of their
just influence in the community, to render profit-
less the means of improvement within their reach,
than the use of ardent spirits as a drink. They
are called on to withstand this practice, as they
regard their honor, and would take their just place
in society. They are under solemn obligations to
give their sanction to every effort for its suppression. They ought to regard as their worst enemies, (though unintentionally such,) as the enemies
of their rights, dignity, and influence, the men
who desire to flood city and country with distilled
poison. I lately visited a flourishing village, and
on expressing to one of the respected inhabitants
the pleasure I felt in witnessing so many signs
of progress, he replied, that one of the causes
of the prosperity I witnessed, was the disuse
of ardent spirits by the people. And this refor-

mation we may be assured wrought something higher than outward prosperity. In almost every family so improved, we cannot doubt that the capacities of the parent for intellectual and moral improvement were enlarged, and the means of education made more effectual to the child. I call on working men to take hold of the cause of temperance as peculiarly *their* cause. These remarks are the more needed, in consequence of the efforts made far and wide, to annul at the present moment a recent law for the suppression of the sale of ardent spirits in such quantities as favor intemperance. I know, that there are intelligent and good men, who believe, that, in enacting this law, government transcended its limits, left its true path, and established a precedent for legislative interference with all our pursuits and pleasures. No one here looks more jealously on government than myself. But I maintain, that this is a case which stands by itself, which can be confounded with no other, and on which government from its very nature and end is peculiarly bound to act. Let it never be forgotten, that the great end of government, its highest function, is, not to make roads, grant charters, originate improvements, but to prevent or repress Crimes against individual rights and social order. For this end it ordains a penal code, erects prisons, and inflicts fearful punishments. Now if it be true, that a vast proportion of the crimes, which government is instituted to prevent and repress, have their origin in the use of ardent spirits ; if our poor-houses, work-houses, jails and penitentiaries are tenanted in a great degree by those, whose first and chief impulse to crime came from the distillery and dram-shop ; if murder and theft, the most fearful outrages on property and life, are most frequently the issues and consummation of intemperance, is not government bound to restrain by legislation the vending of the stimulus to these terrible social wrongs ? Is government never to act as a parent, never to remove the causes or occasion of wrong doing ? Has it but one instrument for repressing crime, namely, public, infamous, punishment, an evil only inferior to crime ? Is government a usurper, does it wander beyond its sphere, by imposing restraints on an article, which does no imaginable good, which can plead no benefit conferred on body or mind, which unfits the citizen for the discharge of his duty to his country, and which, above all, stirs up men to the perpetration of most of the crimes, from which it is the highest and most solemn office of government to protect society ?

I come now to another important measure of self-culture, and this is, intercourse with superior minds. I have insisted on our own activity as essential to our progress ; but we were not made to live or advance alone. Society is as needful to us as air or food. A child doomed to utter loneliness, grow'ng up without sight or sound of human beings, would not put forth equal power with many brutes ; and a man, never brought into contact with minds superior to his own, will probably run one and the same dull round of thought and action to the end of life.

It is chiefly through books that we enjoy intercourse with superior minds, and these invaluable means of communication are in the reach of all. In the best books, great men talk to us, give us their most precious thoughts, and pour their souls into ours. God be thanked for books. They are the voices of the distant and the dead, and make us heirs of the spiritual life of past ages. Books are the true levellers. They give to all, who will faithfully use them, the society, the spiritual presence of the best and greatest of our race. No matter how poor I am. No matter though the prosperous of my own time will not enter my obscure dwelling. If the Sacred Writers will enter and take up their abode under my roof, if Milton will cross my threshold to sing to me of Paradise, and Shakspeare to open to me the worlds of imagination and the workings of the human heart, and Franklin to enrich me with his practical wisdom, I shall not pine for want of intellectual companionship, and I may become a cultivated man though excluded from what is called the best society in the place where I live.

To make this means of culture effectual, a man
must select good books, such as have been written
by right minded and strong minded men, real
thinkers, who instead of diluting by repetition
what others say, have something to say for themselves, and write to give relief to full earnest
souls; and these works must not be skimmed over
for amusement, but read with fixed attention and
a reverential love of truth. In selecting books,
we may be aided much by those who have studied
more than ourselves. But, after all, it is best to
be determined in this particular a good deal by
our own tastes. The best books for a man are not
always those which the wise recommend, but oftener
those which meet the peculiar wants, the natural
thirst of his mind, and therefore awaken interest
and rivet thought. And here it may be well to
observe, not only in regard to books but in other respects, that self-culture must vary with the individual. All means do not equally suit us all. A man
must unfold himself freely, and should respect the
peculiar gifts or biasses by which nature has distinguished him from others. Self-culture does not
demand the sacrifice of individuality. It does not
regularly apply an established machinery, for the
sake of torturing every man into one rigid shape,
called perfection. As the human countenance,
with the same features in us all, is diversified
without end in the race, and is never the same in
any two individuals, so the human soul, with the

same grand powers and laws, expands into an infinite variety of forms, and would be wofully stinted by modes of culture requiring all men to learn the same lesson or to bend to the same rules.

I know how hard it is to some men, especially to those who spend much time in manual labor, to fix attention on books. Let them strive to overcome the difficulty, by choosing subjects of deep interest, or by reading in company with those whom they love. Nothing can supply the place of books. They are cheering or soothing companions in solitude, illness, affliction. The wealth of both continents would not compensate for the good they impart. Let every man, if possible, gather some good books under his roof, and obtain access for himself and family to some social library. Almost any luxury should be sacrificed to this.

One of the very interesting features of our times, is the multiplication of books, and their dis-distribution through all conditions of society. At a small expense, a man can now possess himself of the most precious treasures of English literature. Books, once confined to a few by their costliness, are now accessible to the multitute ; and in this way a change of habits is going on in society, highly favorable to the culture of the people. Instead of depending on casual rumor and loose conversation for most of their knowledge and objects of thought; instead of forming their judgments ·in crowds, and receiving their chief excitement from the voice of neighbors, men are now learning to study and reflect alone, to follow out subjects continuously, to determine for themselves what shall engage their minds, and to call to their aid the knowledge, original views, and reasonings of men of all countries and ages ; and the results must be, a deliberateness and independence of judgment, and a thoroughness and extent of information, unknown in former times. The diffusion of these silent teachers, books, through the whole community, is to work greater effects than artillery, machinery, and legislation. Its peaceful agency is to supersede stormy revolutions. The culture, which it is to spread, whilst an unspeakable good to the individual, is also to become the stability of nations.

Another important means of self-culture, is to free ourselves from the power of human opinion and example, except as far as this is sanctioned by our own deliberate judgment. We are all prone to keep the level of those we live with, to repeat their words, and dress our minds as well as bodies after their fashion ; and hence the spiritless tameness of our characters and lives. Our greatest danger, is not from the grossly wicked around us, but from the worldly, unreflecting multitude, who are borne along as a stream by foreign impulse, and bear us along with them. Even the influence of superior minds may harm us, by bowing us to servile acquiescence and damping our spiritual activity. The great use of intercourse with other minds, is to stir up our own, to whet our appetite for truth, to carry our thoughts beyond their old tracks. We need connexions with great thinkers to make us thinkers too. One of the chief arts of self-culture, is to unite the childlike teachableness, which gratefully welcomes light from every human being who can give it, with manly resistance of opinions however current, of influences however generally revered, which do not approve themselves to our deliberate judgment. You ought indeed patiently and conscientiously to strengthen your reason by other men's intelligence, but you must not prostrate it before them. Especially if there springs up within you any view of God's word or universe, any sentiment or aspiration which seems to you of a higher order than what you meet abroad, give reverent heed to it ; enquire into it earnestly, solemnly. Do not trust it blindly, for it may be an illusion ; but it may be the Divinity moving within you, a new revelation, not supernatural but still most precious, of truth or duty ; and if after enquiry it so appear, then let no clamor, or scorn, or desertion turn you from it. Be true to your own highest convictions. Intimations from our own souls of something more perfect than others teach, if faithfully followed, give us a consciousness of spiritual force and progress, never experienced by the vulgar of high life or low life, who march, as they are drilled, to the step of their times.

Some, I know, will wonder, that I should think the mass of the people capable of such intimations and glimpses of truth, as I have just supposed. These are commonly thought to be the prerogative of men of genius, who seem to be born to give law to the minds of the multitude. Undoubtedly nature has her nobility, and sends forth a few to be eminently " lights of the world." But it is also true that a portion of the same divine fire is given to all ; for the many could not receive with a loving reverence the quickening influences of the few, were there not essentially the same spiritual life in both. The minds of the multitude are not masses of passive matter, created to receive impressions unresistingly from abroad. They are not wholly shaped by foreign instruction ; but have a native force, a spring of thought in themselves. Even the child's mind outruns its lessons, and overflows in questionings which bring the wisest to a stand. Even the child starts the great problems, which philosophy has labored to solve for ages. But on this subject I cannot now enlarge. Let me only say, that the power of original thought is particularly manifested in those, who thirst for progress, who are bent on unfolding their whole nature. A man who wakes up to the consciousness of having been created for progress and perfection, looks with new eyes on himself

and on the world in which he lives. This great
truth stirs the soul from its depths, breaks up old
associations of ideas, and establishes new ones,
just as a mighty agent of chemistry, brought into
contact with natural substances, dissolves the old
affinities which had bound their particles together,
and arranges them anew. This truth particularly
aids us to penetrate the mysteries of human life.
By revealing to us the end of our being, it helps
us to comprehend more and more the wonderful,
the infinite system, to which we belong. A man in
the common walks of life, who has faith in perfection, in the unfolding of the human spirit, as the
great purpose of God, possesses more the secret
of the universe, perceives more the harmonies
or mutual adaptations of the world without and
the world within him, is a wiser interpreter of
Providence, and reads nobler lessons of duty in
the events which pass before him, than the pro-
foundest philosopher who wants this grand cen-
tral truth. Thus illuminations, inward sugges-
tions, are not confined to a favored few, but visit
all who devote themselves to a generous self-
culture.

Another means of Self-culture may be found by
every man in his Condition or Occupation, be it
what it may. Had I time, I might go through all
conditions of life, from the most conspicuous to
the most obscure, and might show how each furn-

ishes continual aids to improvement. But I will take one example, and that is, of a man living by manual labor. This may be made the means of Self-culture. For instance, in almost all labor, a man exchanges his strength for an equivalent in the form of wages, purchase-money, or some other product. In other words, labor is a system of contracts, bargains, imposing mutual obligations. Now the man, who, in working, no matter in what way, strives perpetually to fulfil his obligations thoroughly, to do his whole work faithfully, to be honest not because honesty is the best policy, but for the sake of justice, and that he may render to every man his due, such a laborer is continually building up in himself one of the greatest principles of morality and religion. Every blow on the anvil, on the earth, or whatever material he works upon, contributes something to the perfection of his nature.

Nor is this all. Labor is a school of benevolence as well as justice. A man to support himself must serve others. He must do or produce something for their comfort or gratification. This is one of the beautiful ordinations of Providence, that, to get a living, a man must be useful. Now this usefulness ought to be an end in his labor as truly as to earn his living. He ought to think of the benefit of those he works for, as well as of his own ; and in so doing, in desiring amidst his sweat and toil to serve others as well as himself,

he is exercising and growing in benevolence, as
truly as if he were distributing bounty with a
large hand to the poor. Such a motive hallows
and dignifies the commonest pursuit. It is strange,
that laboring men do not think more of the vast
usefulness of their toils, and take a benevolent
pleasure in them on this account. This beautiful
city, with its houses, furniture, markets, public
walks, and numberless accommodations, has grown
up under the hands of artizans and other laborers,
and ought they not to take a disinterested joy in
their work? One would think, that a carpenter
or mason, on passing a house which he had
reared, would say to himself, " this work of mine
is giving comfort and enjoyment every day and
hour to a family, and will continue to be a kindly
shelter, a domestic gathering-place, an abode of
affection, for a century or more after I sleep in
the dust;" and ought not a generous satisfaction
to spring up at the thought? It is by thus inter-
weaving goodness with common labors, that we
give it strength and make it a habit of the soul.

Again. Labor may be so performed as to be a
high impulse to the mind. Be a man's vocation
what it may, his rule should be to do its duties
perfectly, to do the best he can, and thus to make
perpetual progress in his art. In other words,
Perfection should be proposed; and this I urge
not only for its usefulness to society, nor for the
sincere pleasure which a man takes in seeing a

work well done. This is an important means of
Self-culture. In this way the idea of Perfection
takes root in the mind, and spreads far beyond the
man's trade. He gets a tendency towards com-
pleteness in whatever he undertakes. Slack,
slovenly performance in any department of life is
more apt to offend him. His standard of action
rises, and every thing is better done for his
thoroughness in his common vocation.

There is one circumstance attending all conditions of life, which may and ought to be turned to
the use of self-culture. Every condition, be it
what it may, has hardships, hazards, pains. We
try to escape them ; we pine for a sheltered lot,
for a smooth path, for cheering friends, and un-
broken success. But providence ordains storms,
disasters, hostilities, sufferings ; and the great question, whether we shall live to any purpose or not,
whether we shall grow strong in mind and heart,
or be weak and pitiable, depends on nothing so
much as on our use of these adverse circumstances.
Outward evils are designed to school our passions,
and to rouse our faculties and virtues into intenser
action. Sometimes they seem to create new powers. Difficulty is the element, and resistance the
true work of a man. Self-culture never goes on
so fast, as when embarrassed circumstances, the
opposition of men or the elements, unexpected
changes of the times, or other forms of suffering,
instead of disheartning, throw us on our inward

resources, turn us for strength to God, clear up to us the great purpose of life, and inspire calm resolution. No greatness or goodness is worth much, unless tried in these fires. Hardships are not on this account to be sought for. They come fast enough of themselves, and we are in more danger of sinking under, than of needing them. But when God sends them, they are noble means of self-culture, and as such, let us meet and bear them cheerfully. Thus all parts of our condition may be pressed into the service of self-improvement.

I have time to consider but one more means of self-culture. We find it in our Free Government, in our Political relations and duties. It is a great benefit of free institutions, that they do much to awaken and keep in action a nation's mind. We are told, that the education of the multitude is necessary to the support of a republic; but it is equally true, that a republic is a powerful means of educating the multitude. It is the people's University. In a free state, solemn responsibilities are imposed on every citizen; great subjects are to be discussed; great interests to be decided. The individual is called to determine measures affecting the well-being of millions and the destinies of posterity. He must consider not only the internal relations of his native land, but its connexion with foreign states, and judge of a policy which touches the whole civilized world. He is called by his participation in the national sovereignty, to cherish public spirit, a regard to the general weal. A man who purposes to discharge faithfully these obligations, is carrying on a generous self-culture. The great public questions, which divide opinion around him and provoke earnest discussion, of necessity invigorate his intellect, and accustom him to look beyond himself. He grows up to a robustness, force, enlargement of mind, unknown under despotic rule.

It may be said that I am describing what free institutious ought to do for the character of the individual, not their actual effects; and the objection, I must own, is too true. Our institutions do not cultivate us, as they might and should; and the chief cause of the failure is plain. It is the strength of party spirit; and so blighting is its influence, so fatal to self-culture, that I feel myself bound to warn every man against it, who has any desire of improvement. I do not tell you it will destroy your country. It wages a worse war against yourselves. Truth, justice, candor, fair dealing, sound judgment, self-control, and kind affections are its natural and perpetual prey.

I do not say, that you must take no side in politics. The parties which prevail around you differ in character, principles, and spirit, though far less than the exaggeration of passion affirms; and, as far as conscience allows, a man should support that,

which he thinks best. In one respect, however,
all parties agree. They all foster that pestilent
spirit, which I now condemn. In all of them,
party spirit rages. Associate men together for
a common cause, be it good or bad, and array
against them a body resolutely pledged to an
opposite interest, and a new passion, quite distinct from the original sentiment which brought
them together, a fierce, fiery zeal, consisting
chiefly of aversion to those who differ from
them, is roused within them into fearful activity. Human nature seems incapable of a
stronger, more unrelenting passion. It is hard
enough for an individual, when contending all
alone for an interest or an opinion, to keep down
his pride, wilfulness, love of victory, anger and
other personal feelings. But let him join a multitude in the same warfare, and, without singular
self-control, he receives into his single breast the
vehemence, obstinacy and vindictiveness of all.
The triumph of his party becomes immeasurably
dearer to him than the principle, true or false,
which was the original ground of division. The
conflict becomes a struggle not for principle but
for power, for victory ; and the desperateness,
the wickedness of such struggles, is the great
burden of history. In truth, it matters little
what men divide about, whether it be a foot of
land or precedence in a procession. Let them
but begin to fight for it, and self-will, ill-will, the

rage for victory, the dread of mortification and defeat, makes the trifle as weighty as a matter of life and death. The Greek or Eastern empire was shaken to its foundation by parties, which differed only about the merits of charioteers at the amphitheatre. Party spirit is singularly hostile to moral independence. A man, in proportion as he drinks into it, sees, hears, judges by the senses and understandings of his party. He surrenders the freedom of a man, the right of using and speaking his own mind, and echoes the applauses or maledictions, with which the leaders or passionate partizans see fit that the country should ring. On all points parties are to be distrusted ; but on no one so much as on the character of opponents. These, if you may trust what you hear, are always men without principle and truth, devoured by selfishness, and thirsting for their own elevation, though on their country's ruin. When I was young, I was accustomed to hear pronounced with abhorrence, almost with execration, the names of men, who are now hailed by their former foes as the champions of grand principles and as worthy of the highest public trusts. This lesson of early experience, which later years have corroborated, will never be forgotten.

Of our present political divisions I have of course nothing to say. But among the current topics of party, there are certain accusations and recriminations, grounded on differences of social condition, which seem to me so unfriendly to the improvement of individuals and the community, that I ask the privilege of giving them a moment's notice. On one side we are told, that the rich are disposed to trample on the poor ; and on the other, that the poor look with evil eye and hostile purpose on the possessions of the rich. These outcries seem to me alike devoid of truth and alike demoralizing. As for the rich, who constitute but a handful of our population, who possess not one peculiar privilege, and, what is more, who possess comparatively little of the property of the country, it is wonderful, that they should be objects of alarm. The vast and ever-growing property of this country, where is it ? Locked up in a few hands ? hoarded in a few strong boxes ? It is diffused like the atmosphere, and almost as variable, changing hands with the seasons, shifting from rich to poor, not by the violence but by the industry and skill of the latter class. The wealth of the rich is as a drop in the ocean ; and it is a well known fact, that those men among us, who are noted for their opulence, exert hardly any political power on the community. That the rich do their whole duty ; that they adopt, as they should, the great object of the social state, which is the elevation of the people in intelligence, character, and condition, cannot be pretended ; but that they feel for the physical sufferings of their brethren, that they stretch out liberal hands for the succor of the poor and for the support of useful public institutions, cannot be denied. Among them are admirable specimens of humanity. There is no warrant for holding them up to suspicion as the people's foes.

Nor do I regard as less calumnious the outcry against the working classes, as if they were aiming at the subversion of property. When we think of the general condition and character of this part of our population, when we recollect, that they were born and have lived amidst schools and churches, that they have been brought up to profitable industry, that they enjoy many of the accommodations of life, that most of them hold a measure of property and are hoping for more, that they possess unprecedented means of bettering their lot, that they are bound to comfortable homes by strong domestic affections, that they are able to give their children an education which places within their reach the prizes of the social state, that they are trained to the habits, and familiarized to the advantages of a high civilization; when we recollect these things, can we imagine that they are so insanely blind to their interests, so deaf to the calls of justice and religion, so profligately thoughtless of the peace and safety of their families, as to be prepared to make a wreck of social order, for the sake of dividing among themselves the spoils of the rich, which would not support the community for a month. Undoubtedly

tual calumnies. Let not class array itself against class, where all have a common interest. One way of provoking men to crime is to suspect them of criminal designs. We do not secure our property against the poor, by accusing them of schemes of universal robbery ; nor render the rich better friends of the community, by fixing on them the brand of hostility to the people. Of all parties, those founded on different social conditions are the most pernicious ; and in no country on earth are they so groundless as in our own.

Among the best people, especially among the more religious, there are some, who, through disgust with the violence and frauds of parties, withdraw themselves from all political action. Such, I conceive, do wrong. God has placed them in the relations, and imposed on them the duties of citizens ; and they are no more authorized to shrink from these duties than from those of sons, husbands, or fathers. They owe a great debt to their country, and must discharge it by giving support to what they deem the best men and the best measures. Nor let them say, that they can do nothing. Every good man, if faithful to his convictions, benefits his country. All parties are kept in check by the spirit of the better portion of people, whom they contain. Leaders are always compelled to ask what their party will bear, and to modify their measures, so as not to shock the men of principle within their ranks. A good man, not tamely subservient to the body with which he acts, but judging it impartially, criticising it freely, bearing testimony against its evils, and withholding his support from wrong, does good to those around him, and is cultivating generously his own mind.

I respectfully counsel those, whom I address, to take part in the politics of their country. These are the true discipline of a people, and do much for their education. I counsel you to labor for a clear understanding of the subjects which agitate the community, to make them your study, instead of wasting your leisure in vague, passionate talk about them. The time thrown away by the mass of the people on the rumors of the day, might, if better spent, give them a good acquaintance with the constitution, laws, history and interests of their country, and thus establish them in those great principles by which particular measures are to be determined. In proportion as the people thus improve themselves, they will cease to be the tools of designing politicians. Their intelligence, not their passions and jealousies, will be addressed by those who seek their votes. They will exert, not a nominal, but a real influence on the government and the destinies of the country, and at the same time will forward their own growth in truth and virtue.

I ought not to quit this subject of politics, considered as a means of self-culture, without speaking of newspapers ; because these form the chief reading of the bulk of the people. They are the

literature of multitudes. Unhappily their importance is not understood ; their bearing on the intellectual and moral cultivation of the community,
little thought of. A newspaper ought to be conducted by one of our most gifted men, and its
income should be such as to enable him to secure
the contributions of men as gifted as himself. But
we must take newspapers as they are ; and a man,
anxious for self-culture, may turn them to account,
if he will select the best within his reach. He
should exclude from his house such as are venom-
ous or scurrilous, as he would a pestilence. He
should be swayed in his choice, not merely by the
ability with which a paper is conducted, but still
more by its spirit, by its justice, fairness and
steady adherence to great principles. Especially,
if he would know the truth, let him hear both
sides. Let him read the defence as well as the
attack. Let him not give his ear to one party exclusively. We condemn ourselves, when we listen
to reproaches thrown on an individual and turn
away from his exculpation ; and is it just to read
continual, unsparing invective against large masses
of men, and refuse them the opportunity of justi-
fying themselves ?

A new class of daily papers has sprung up in our
country, sometimes called cent papers, and designed
for circulation among those who cannot afford cost-
lier publications. My interest in the working class
induced me sometime ago to take one of these,

and I was gratified to find it not wanting in useful matter. Two things however gave me pain. The advertising columns were devoted very much to patent medicines ; and when I considered that a laboring man's whole fortune is his health, I could not but lament, that so much was done to seduce him to the use of articles, more fitted, I fear, to undermine than to restore his constitution. I was also shocked by accounts of trials in the police court. These were written in a style adapted to the most uncultivated minds, and intended to turn into matters of sport the most painful and humiliating events of life. Were the newspapers of the rich to attempt to extract amusement from the vices and miseries of the poor, a cry would be raised against them, and very justly. But is it not something worse, that the poorer classes themselves should seek occasions of laughter and merriment in the degradation, the crimes, the woes, the punishments of their brethren, of those who are doomed to bear like themselves the heaviest burdens of life, and who have sunk under the temptations of poverty ? Better go to the hospital, and laugh over the wounds and writhings of the sick or the ravings of the insane, than amuse ourselves with brutal excesses and infernal passions, which not only expose the criminal to the crushing penalties of human laws, but incur the displeasure of Heaven, and, if not repented of, will be followed by the fearful retribution of the life to come.

One important topic remains. That great means of self-improvement, Christianity, is yet untouched, and its greatness forbids me now to approach it. I will only say, that if you study Christianity in its original records and not in human creeds ; if you consider its clear revelations of God, its life-giving promises of pardon and spiritual strength, its correspondence to man's reason, conscience and best affections, and its adaptation to his wants, sorrows, anxieties and fears ; if you consider the strength of its proofs, the purity of its precepts, the divine greatness of the character of its author, and the immortality which it opens before us, you will feel yourselves bound to welcome it joyfully, gratefully, as affording aids and incitements to self-culture, which would vainly be sought in all other means.

I have thus presented a few of the means of self-culture. The topics, now discussed, will I hope suggest others to those who have honored me with their attention, and create an interest which will extend beyond the present hour. I owe it however to truth to make one remark. I wish to raise no unreasonable hopes. I must say then, that the means, now recommended to you, though they will richly reward every man of every age who will faithfully use them, will yet not produce their full and happiest effect, except in cases where early education has prepared the mind for future improvement. They, whose childhood has been neglected, though they may make progress in future life, can hardly repair the loss of their first years ; and I say this, that we may all be excited to save our children from this loss, that we may prepare them, to the extent of our power, for an effectual use of all the means of self-culture, which adult age may bring with it. With these views, I ask you to look with favor on the recent exertions of our legislature and of private citizens, in behalf of our public schools, the chief hope of our country. The legislature has of late appointed a board of education, with a secretary, who is to devote his whole time to the improvement of public schools. An individual more fitted to this responsible office, than the gentleman who now fills it,* cannot, I believe, be found in our community ; and if his labors shall be crowned with success, he will earn a title to the gratitude of the good people of this State, unsurpassed by that of any other living citizen. Let me also recall to your minds a munificent individual,† who, by a generous donation, has encouraged the legislature to resolve on the establishment of one or more institutions called Normal Schools, the object of which is, to prepare accomplished teachers of youth, a work, on which the progress of education depends more than on any other measure. The efficient friends of education are the true benefactors of their

---

* Horace Mann, Esq.         † Edmund Dwight, Esq.

country, and their names deserve to be handed down to that posterity, for whose highest wants they are generously providing.

There is another mode of advancing education in our whole country, to which I ask your particular attention. You are aware of the vast extent and value of the public lands of the Union. By annual sales of these, large amounts of money are brought into the national treasury, which are applied to the current expenses of the Government. For this application there is no need. In truth, the country has received detriment from the excess of its revenues. Now, I ask, why shall not the public lands be consecrated, (in whole or in part, as the case may require,) to the education of the people? This measure would secure at once what the country most needs, that is, able, accomplished, quickening teachers of the whole rising generation. The present poor remuneration of instructers is a dark omen, and the only real obstacle which the cause of education has to contend with. We need for our schools gifted men, and women, worthy, by their intelligence and their moral power, to be entrusted with a nation's youth ; and to gain these we must pay them liberally, as well as afford other proofs of the consideration in which we hold them. In the present state of the country, when so many paths of wealth and promotion are opened, superior men cannot be won to an office so responsible and la-

borious as that of teaching, without stronger in-
ducements than are now offered, except in some
of our large cities. The office of instructer ought
to rank and be recompensed as one of the most
honorable in society ; and I see not how this is
to be done, at least in our day, without appro-
priating to it the public domain. This is the people's property, and the only part of their property
which is likely to be soon devoted to the support
of a high order of institutions for public education. This object, interesting to all classes of
society, has peculiar claims on those whose means
of improvement are restricted by narrow circumstances. The mass of the people should devote
themselves to it as one man, should toil for it with
one soul. Mechanics, Farmers, Laborers ! Let
the country echo with your united cry, " The
Public Lands for Education." Send to the public
councils men who will plead this cause with
power. No party triumphs, no trades-unions, no
associations, can so contribute to elevate you as
the measure now proposed. Nothing but a higher
education can raise you in influence and true dignity. The resources of the public domain, wisely
applied for successive generations to the culture of
society and of the individual, would create a new
people, would awaken through this community intellectual and moral energies, such as the records
of no country display, and as would command the
respect and emulation of the civilized world. In

9

this grand object, the working men of all parties, and in all divisions of the land, should join with an enthusiasm not to be withstood. They should separate it from all narrow and local strifes. They should not suffer it to be mixed up with the schemes of politicians. In it, they and their children have an infinite stake. May they be true to themselves, to posterity, to their country, to freedom, to the cause of mankind.

III. I am aware that the whole doctrine of this discourse will meet opposition. There are not a few who will say to me, " What you tell us sounds well; but it is impracticable. Men, who dream in their closets, spin beautiful theories ; but actual life scatters them, as the wind snaps the cobweb. You would have all men to be cultivated ; but necessity wills that most men shall work ; and which of the two is likely to prevail. A weak sentimentality may shrink from the truth ; still it *is* true, that most men were made, not for self-culture, but for toil."

I have put the objection into strong language, that we may all look it fairly in the face. For one I deny its validity. Reason as well as sentiment rises up against it. The presumption is certainly very strong, that the All-wise Father, who has given to every human being, reason and conscience and affection, intended that these should be unfolded ; and it is hard to believe, that He,

who, by conferring this nature on all men, has
made all his children, has destined the great majority to wear out a life of drudgery and unimproving toil, for the benefit of a few. God cannot
have made spiritual beings to be dwarfed. In the
body we see no organs created to shrivel by disuse; much less are the powers of the soul given to
be locked up in perpetual lethargy.

Perhaps it will be replied, that the purpose of
the Creator is to be gathered, not from theory, but
from facts ; and that it is a plain fact, that the
order and prosperity of society, which God must
be supposed to intend, require from the multitude
the action of their hands and not the improvement
of their minds. I reply, that a social order, de-
manding the sacrifice of the mind, is very suspi-
cious, that it cannot indeed be sanctioned by the
Creator. Were I, on visiting a strange country,
to see the vast majority of the people maimed,
crippled, and bereft of sight, and were I told that
social order required this mutilation, I should say,
Perish this order. Who would not think his understanding as well as best feelings insulted, by
hearing this spoken of as the intention of God.
Nor ought we to look with less aversion on a
social system, which can only be upheld by crip-
pling and blinding the Minds of the people.

But to come nearer to the point. Are labor
and self-culture irreconcileable to each other. In
the first place, we have seen that a man, in the

midst of labor, may and ought to give himself to
the most important improvements, that he may
cultivate his sense of justice, his benevolence, and
the desire of perfection. Toil is the school for
these high principles ; and we have here a strong
presumption, that, in other respects, it does not
necessarily blight the soul. Next we have seen,
that the most fruitful sources of truth and wisdom are not books, precious as they are, but
experience and observation ; and these belong
to all conditions. It is another important consideration, that almost all labor demands intellectual activity, and is best carried on by those
who invigorate their minds; so that the two interests, toil and self-culture, are friends to each
other. It is Mind, after all, which does the work
of the world, so that the more there is of mind,
the more work will be accomplished. A man, in
proportion as he is intelligent, makes a given force
accomplish a greater task, makes skill take the
place of muscles, and, with less labor, gives a
better product. Make men intelligent and they
become inventive. They find shorter processes.
Their knowledge of nature helps them to turn its
laws to account, to understand the substances on
which they work, and to seize on useful hints,
which experience continually furnishes. It is
among workmen, that some of the most useful ma-
chines have been contrived. Spread education,
and, as the history of this country shows, there

will be no bounds to useful inventions. You think, that a man without culture will do all the better what you call the drudgery of life. Go then to the Southern plantation. There the slave is brought up to be a mere drudge. He is robbed of the rights of a man, his whole spiritual nature is starved, that he may work and do nothing but work : and in that slovenly agriculture, in that worn out soil, in the rude state of the mechanic arts, you may find a comment on your doctrine, that by degrading men you make them more productive laborers.

But it is said, that any considerable education lifts men above their work, makes them look with disgust on their trades as mean and low, makes drudgery intolerable. I reply, that a man becomes interested in labor , just in proportion as the mind works with the hands. An enlightened farmer, who understands agricultural chemistry, the laws of vegetation, the structure of plants, the properties of manures, the influences of climate, who looks intelligently on his work and brings his knowledge to bear on exigences, is a much more cheerful as well as more dignified laborer, than the peasant, whose mind is akin to the clod on which he treads, and whose whole life is the same dull, unthinking, unimproving toil. But this is not all. Why is it, I ask, that we call manual labor low, that we associate with it the idea of meanness, and think that an intelligent people must scorn it ? The great reason is, that, in most countries, so few intelligent people have been engaged in it. Once let cultivated men plough and dig and follow the commonest labors, and ploughing, digging and trades will cease to be mean. It is the man who determines the dignity of the occupation, not the occupation which measures the dignity of the man. Physicians and surgeons perform operations less cleanly than fall to the lot of most mechanics. I have seen a distinguished chemist covered with dust like a laborer. Still these men were not degraded. Their intelligence gave dignity to their work, and so our laborers, once educated, will give dignity to their toils.—Let me add, that I see little difference in point of dignity, between the various vocations of men. When I see a clerk, spending his days in adding figures perhaps merely copying, or a teller of a bank counting money, or a merchant selling shoes and hides, I cannot see in these occupations greater respectableness than in making leather, shoes, or furniture. I do not see in them greater intellectual activity than in several trades. A man in the fields seems to have more chances of improvement in his work, than a man behind the counter, or a man driving the quill. It is the sign of a narrow mind, to imagine, as many seem to do, that there is a repugnance between the plain, coarse exterior of a laborer and mental culture, especially the more

refining culture. The laborer, under his dust and
sweat, carries the grand elements of humanity,
and he may put forth its highest powers. I doubt
not, there is as genuine enthusiasm in the contem-
plation of nature and in the perusal of works of
genius, under a homespun garb as under finery.
We have heard of a distinguished author, who
never wrote so well, as when he was full dressed
for company. But profound thought and poetical
inspiration have most generally visited men, when,
from narrow circumstances or negligent habits,
the rent coat and shaggy face have made them
quite unfit for polished saloons. A man may see
truth, and may be thrilled with beauty, in one cos-
tume or dwelling as well as another; and he
should respect himself the more for the hardships,
under which his intellectual force has been devel-
oped.

But it will be asked, how can the laboring
classes find time for self-culture. I answer, as I
have already intimated, that an earnest purpose
finds time or makes time. It seizes on spare mo-
ments, and turns larger fragments of leisure to
golden account. A man, who follows his calling
with industry and spirit, and uses his earnings
economically, will always have some portion of
the day at command ; and it is astonishing, how
fruitful of improvement a short season becomes,
when eagerly seized and faithfully used. It has
often been observed, that they, who have most

time at their disposal, profit by it least. A single
hour in the day, steadily given to the study of an
interesting subject, brings unexpected accumulations of knowledge. The improvement made by
well disposed pupils, in many of our country
schools, which are open but three months in the
year, and in our Sunday schools, which are kept
but one or two hours in the week, show what can
be brought to pass by slender means. The affections, it is said, sometimes crowd years into mo-
ments, and the intellect has something of the
same power. Volumes have not only been read,
but written, in flying journeys. I have known a
man of vigorous intellect, who had enjoyed few
advantages of early education, and whose mind
was almost engrossed by the details of an extensive business, but who composed a book of much
original thought, in steamboats and on horseback,
while visiting distant customers. The succession
of the seasons gives to many of the working class
opportunities for intellectual improvement. The
winter brings leisure to the husbandman, and winter evenings to many laborers in the city. Above
all, in Christian countries, the seventh day is
released from toil. The seventh part of the year,
no small portion of existence, may be given by
almost every one to intellectual and moral culture.
Why is it that Sunday is not made a more effectual
means of improvement ? Undoubtedly the seventh day is to have a religious character ; but

religion connects itself with all the great subjects
of human thought, and leads to and aids the study
of all. God is in nature. God is in history. Instruction in the works of the Creator, so as to
reveal his perfection in their harmony, benefi-
cence and grandeur ; instruction in the histories
of the church and the world, so as to show in all
events his moral government, and to bring out the
great moral lessons in which human life abounds ;
instruction in the lives of philanthropists, of saints,
of men eminent for piety and virtue ; all these
branches of teaching enter into religion, and are
appropriate to Sunday ; and through these, a vast
amount of knowledge may be given to the people.
Sunday ought not to remain the dull and fruitless
season, that it now is to multitudes. It may be
clothed with a new interest and a new sanctity.
It may give a new impulse to the nation's soul.—I
have thus shown, that time may be found for improvement; and the fact is, that among our most
improved people, a considerable part consists of
persons, who pass the greatest portion of every day
at the desk, in the counting room, or in some
other sphere, chained to tasks which have very
little tendency to expand the mind. In the progress of society, with the increase of machinery,
and with other aids which intelligence and philan-
thropy will multiply, we may expect that more
and more time will be redeemed from manual
labor, for intellectual and social occupations.

10

But some will say, " Be it granted that the
working classes may find some leisure ; should
they not be allowed to spend it in relaxation ? Is
it not cruel, to summon them from toils of the
hand to toils of the mind ? They have earned
pleasure by the day's toil and ought to partake
it." Yes, let them have pleasure. Far be it
from me to dry up the fountains, to blight the
spots of verdure, where they refresh themselves
after life's labors. But I maintain, that self-culture
multiplies and increases their pleasures, that it
creates new capacities of enjoyment, that it saves
their leisure from being, what it too often is, dull
and wearisome, that it saves them from rushing for
excitement to indulgences destructive to body and
soul. It is one of the great benefits of self-improvement, that it raises a people above the gratifications of the brute, and gives them pleasures
worthy of men. In consequence of the present
intellectual culture of our country, imperfect as it
is, a vast amount of enjoyment is communicated to
men, women and children, of all conditions, by
books, an enjoyment unknown to ruder times. At
this moment, a number of gifted writers are employed in multiplying entertaining works. Walter
Scott, a name conspicuous among the brightest of
his day, poured out his inexhaustible mind in fictions, at once so sportive and thrilling, that they
have taken their place among the delights of all
civilized nations. How many millions have been

chained to his pages! How many melancholy
spirits has he steeped in forgetfulness of their
cares and sorrows! What multitudes, wearied by
their day's work, have owed some bright evening
hours and balmier sleep to his magical creations !
And not only do fictions give pleasure. In proportion as the mind is cultivated, it takes delight
in history and biography, in descriptions of nature,
in travels, in poetry, and even graver works. Is
the laborer then defrauded of pleasure by improvement ? There is another class of gratifications to which self-culture introduces the mass of
the people. I refer to lectures, discussions, meet-
ings of associations for benevolent and literary
purposes, and to other like methods of passing the
evening, which every year is multiplying among
us. A popular address from an enlightened man,
who has the tact to reach the minds of the people,
is a high gratification, as well as a source of
knowledge. The profound silence in our public
halls, where these lectures are delivered to
crowds, shows that cultivation is no foe to enjoyment.—I have a strong hope, that by the progress
of intelligence, taste and morals among all portions of society, a class of public amusements will
grow up among us, bearing some resemblance to
the theatre, but purified from the gross evils which
degrade our present stage, and which, I trust, will
seal its ruin. Dramatic performances and recita-
tions are means of bringing the mass of the peo-

ple into a quicker sympathy with a writer of genius, to a profounder comprehension of his grand, beautiful, touching conceptions, than can be effected by the reading of the closet. No commentary throws such a light on a great poem or any impassioned work of literature, as the voice of a reader or speaker, who brings to the task a deep feeling of his author and rich and various powers of expression. A crowd, electrified by a sublime thought, or softened into a humanizing sorrow, under such a voice, partake a pleasure at once exquisite and refined ; and I cannot but believe, that this and other amusements, at which the delicacy of woman and the purity of the Christian can take no offence, are to grow up under a higher social culture.—Let me only add, that in proportion as culture spreads among a people, the cheapest and commonest of all pleasures, conversation, increases in delight. This, after all, is the great amusement of life, cheering us round our hearths, often cheering our work, stirring our hearts gently, acting on us like the balmy air or the bright light of heaven, so silently and continually, that we hardly think of its influence. This source of happiness is too often lost to men of all classes for want of knowledge, mental activity, and refinement of feeling ; and do we defraud the laborer of his pleasure, by recommending to him improvements which will place the daily, hourly, blessings of conversation within his reach ?

I have thus considered some of the common objections which start up when the culture of the mass of men is insisted on, as the great end of society. For myself, these objections seem worthy little notice. The doctrine is too shocking to need refutation, that the great majority of human beings, endowed as they are with rational and immortal powers, are placed on earth, simply to toil for their own animal subsistence, and to minister to the luxury and elevation of the few. It is monstrous, it approaches impiety, to suppose that God has placed insuperable barriers to the expansion of the free illimitable soul. True, there are obstructions in the way of improvement. But in this country, the chief obstructions lie, not in our lot, but in ourselves, not in outward hardships, but in our worldly and sensual propensities ; and one proof of this is, that a true self-culture is as little thought of on exchange as in the workshop, as little among the prosperous as among those of narrower conditions. The path to perfection is difficult to men in every lot ; there is no royal road for rich or poor. But difficulties are meant to rouse not discourage. The human spirit is to grow strong by conflict. And how much has it already overcome ! Under what burdens of oppression has it made its way for ages ! What mountains of difficulty has it cleared ! And with all this experience, shall we say, that the progress of the mass of men is to be despaired of, that the.

chains of bodily necessity are too strong and pon-
derous to be broken by the mind, that servile,
unimproving drudgery is the unalterable condition
of the multitude of the human race ?

I conclude with recalling to you the happiest
feature of our age, and that is, the progress of the
mass of the people in intelligence, self-respect,
and all the comforts of life. What a contrast
does the present form with past times! Not many
ages ago, the nation was the property of one man,
and all its interests were staked in perpetual
games of war, for no end but to build up his family, or to bring new territories under his yoke.
Society was divided into two classes, the highborn
and the vulgar, separated from one another by a
great gulph, as impassable as that between the
saved and the lost. The people had no significance as individuals, but formed a mass, a machine, to be wielded at pleasure by their lords.
In war, which was the great sport of the times,
those brave knights, of whose prowess we hear,
cased themselves and their horses in armour, so
as to be almost invulnerable, whilst the common
people on foot were left, without protection, to
be hewn in pieces or trampled down by their bet-
ters. Who, that compares the condition of Europe
a few ages ago, with the present state of the
world, but must bless God for the change. The
grand distinction of modern times is, the emerging

of the people from brutal degradation, the gradual
recognition of their rights, the gradual diffusion
among them of the means of improvement and
happiness, the creation of a new power in the
state, the power of the people. And it is worthy
remark, that this revolution is due in a great
degree to religion, which, in the hands of the
crafty and aspiring, had bowed the multitude to
the dust, but which, in the fulness of time, began
to fulfil its mission of freedom. It was religion,
which, by teaching men their near relation to
God, awakened in them the consciousness of their
importance as individuals. It was the struggle for
religious rights, which opened men's eyes to all
their rights. It was resistance to religious usur-
pation, which led men to withstand political oppression. It was religious discussion, which roused
the minds of all classes to free and vigorous
thought. It was religion, which armed the
martyr and patriot in England against arbitrary
power, which braced the spirits of our fathers
against the perils of the ocean and wilderness,
and sent them to found here the freest and most
equal state on earth.

Let us thank God for what has been gained.
But let us not think every thing gained. Let the
people feel that they have only started in the race.
How much remains to be done! What a vast
amount of ignorance, intemperance, coarseness,
sensuality, may still be found in our community!

What a vast amount of mind is palsied and lost! When we think, that every house might be cheered by intelligence, disinterestedness and refinement, and then remember, in how many houses the higher powers and affections of human nature are buried as in tombs, what a darkness gathers over society. And how few of us are moved by this moral desolation? How few understand, that to raise the depressed, by a wise culture, to the dignity of men, is the highest end of the social state? Shame on us, that the worth of a fellow creature is so little felt.

I would, that I could speak with an awakening voice to the people, of their wants, their privileges, their responsibilities. I would say to them, You cannot, without guilt and disgrace, stop where you are. The past and the present call on you to advance. Let what you have gained be an impulse to something higher. Your nature is too great to be crushed. You were not created what you are, merely to toil, eat, drink and sleep, like the inferior animals. If you will, you can rise. No power in society, no hardship in your condition can depress you, keep you down, in knowledge, power, virtue, influence, but by your own consent. Do not be lulled to sleep by the flatteries which you hear, as if your participation in the national sovereignty made you equal to the noblest of your race. You have many and great deficiencies to be remedied; and the remedy lies, not in the ballot box, not in the exercise of your political powers, but in the faithful education of yourselves and your children. These truths you have often heard and slept over. Awake! Resolve earnestly on Self-culture. Make yourselves worthy of your free institutions, and strengthen and perpetuate them by your intelligence and your virtues.

11

# FRANKLIN LECTURES.

THESE Lectures were instituted in 1831. They were designed to give entertainment and instruction, upon terms so moderate, that every body might attend them. They have been continued, with the exception of one year, every winter since they were founded, and have been always very fully attended. In now publishing the Introductory Lecture to the Course for 1838, the Executive Committee beg leave to give notice, that the Lectures will be continued in succeeding years.

WALTER CHANNING, *Chairman.*

DAVID KIMBALL, *Secretary and Treasurer.*

WALTER CHANNING,
JONATHAN PHILLIPS,
ENOCH HOBART,
WILLIAM BRIGHAM,
LEWIS G. PRAY,
DAVID KIMBALL,
TIMOTHY CLAXTON,
E. P. HARTSHORN,
MICHAEL TOMBS,
WILLIAM C. MARTIN,
JOHN FORD,
FRANCIS BROWN,

*Executive Committee.*